TIBETAN symbols & designs
COLORING BOOK

We give all sorts of things an extra layer of meaning, a symbolic meaning. A white bird in a painting is a dove, but it's also a symbol of peace. Since peace is an idea, it can't be drawn directly, so artists have found a way to convey that idea with a picture of a white bird.

In Tibet, carpets and other fabrics are decorated with guardians, birds, flowers, and designs. Many of the designs have a symbolic meaning like the dove, including the dragons and cranes and lotus blossoms. We've chosen twenty-two Tibetan objects from the collection of the Newark Museum, each of them covered with pictures, for you to color. They are shown as small reproductions on the inside front and back covers. The captions on the pages that follow tell you something about Tibetan symbolism.

The last page of this book is blank so that you can draw and color your own picture. Fill it with snow lions, lotus flowers, and your own symbolic creatures and plants.

NEWARK MUSEUM

Pomegranate kids™

All works are from the Newark Museum.

1. *Shugden* (sitting rug), early twentieth century. Wool weft, cotton warp, natural dyes, 60 x 74 cm (23⅝ x 29⅛ in.). Purchase 2002 Helen McMahon Brady Cutting Fund 2002.1.102.

2. Saddle rug, twentieth century. Wool weft, cotton warp, natural dyes, 57 x 74 cm (22⁷⁄₁₆ x 29⅛ in.). Purchase 2002 Helen McMahon Brady Cutting Fund 2002.1.46A.

3. Ceremonial appliquéd tent (detail), c. 1930s. Cotton, wool, entire length of tent: 457.2 cm (180 in.). Purchase 2002 Helen McMahon Brady Cutting Fund 2002.1.46A.

4. *Shugden* (sitting rug), early twentieth century. Wool, cotton, wool pile, length: 152.4 cm (60 in.). Purchase 1978 Charles W. Engelhard Bequest Fund, 78.137.

5. Lhamo's saddle cover (detail), eighteenth century. Silk, silk brocade, and gilt leather appliqué cover, width of entire cover: 63.5 cm (25 in.). Purchase 1918 George T. Rockwell Collection, 18.132.

6. Tiger rug, late nineteenth-early twentieth centuries. Wool weft, cotton warp, natural dyes, 58 x 80 cm (22¹⁵⁄₁₆ x 31½ in.). Purchase 1959, 59.71.

7. *Pema* (lotus) pattern, early twentieth century. Wool weft, cotton warp, natural dyes, 90 x 179 cm (35⁷⁄₁₆ x 70½ in.). Purchase 2002 Helen McMahon Brady Cutting Fund 2002.1.61.

8. Door curtain rug, early twentieth century. Wool weft, cotton warp, natural dyes, 99 x 204 cm (39 x 80⁵⁄₁₆ in.). Purchase 2002 Helen McMahon Brady Cutting Fund 2002.1.58.

9. *Shugden* (sitting rug), early twentieth century. Wool weft, cotton warp, natural dyes, 54 x 66 cm (21¼ x 26 in.). Purchase 2002 Helen McMahon Brady Cutting Fund 2002.1.119

10. *Kapsho pesar* ("Kapsho's new design"), early twentieth century. Wool weft, cotton warp, natural dyes, 93 x 70 cm (36⅝ x 27⁹⁄₁₆ in.). Purchase 2002 Helen McMahon Brady Cutting Fund 2002.1.85B.

11. Phoenix-pattern *khaden* (bed rug), early twentieth century. Wool weft, cotton warp, natural dyes, 88 x 181 cm (34⅝ x 71¼ in.). Purchase 2002 Helen McMahon Brady Cutting Fund 2002.1.74.

12. Ritual table, side panel (detail), nineteenth century. Painted and coated wood, 28.3 x 69.2 cm (11⅛ x 27¼ in.). Purchase 1975 Thomas L. Raymond Bequest Fund, 75.96.

13. Altar canopy, Ngor Monastery, seventeenth century. Silk tapestry, 195.6 x 251.5 cm (77 x 99 in.). Gift of Jacob E. Henegar, 1986, 86.255.

14. *Gyabney* (cushion cover), early twentieth century. Wool weft, cotton warp, natural and aniline dyes, 42 x 67 cm (16½ x 26⅜ in.). Purchase 2002 Helen McMahon Brady Cutting Fund 2002.1.108A.

15. Banner with "Face of Glory" (detail), nineteenth century. Appliquéd silk brocade and silk-covered horsehair outlining, silk tassels, length of entire banner: 604.8 cm (238⅛ in.). Purchase 1974 C. Suydam Cutting Bequest Fund 74.125.

16. *Khaden* (bed rug), early twentieth century. Wool weft, cotton warp, natural and aniline dyes, 88 x 164 cm (34⅝ x 64⁹⁄₁₆ in.). Purchase 2002 Helen McMahon Brady Cutting Fund 2002.1.87A.

17. *Khaden* (bed rug), early twentieth century. Wool weft, cotton warp, natural dyes, 91 x 149 cm (35¹³⁄₁₆ x 58¹¹⁄₁₆ in.). Purchase 2002 Helen McMahon Brady Cutting Fund 2002.1.82.

18. Saddle rug from Yabshi Phunkang's cavalry, 1920s. Wool weft, cotton warp, 62 x 115 cm (24⅜ x 45¼ in.). Purchase 2002 Helen McMahon Brady Cutting Fund 2002.1.41.

19. *Khaden* (bed rug), early twentieth century. Wool weft, cotton warp, natural dyes, 80 x 148 cm (31½ x 58¼ in.). Purchase 2002 Helen McMahon Brady Cutting Fund 2002.1.88.

20. Throne backrest, early twentieth century. Cotton weft, cotton warp, natural dyes, 82 x 84 cm (32¼ x 33¹⁄₁₆ in.). Purchase 2002 Helen McMahon Brady Cutting Fund 2002.1.38.

21. *Pema chakdro* ("lotus in iron lockets") pattern, early twentieth century. Wool weft, cotton warp, natural dyes, 73 x 131 cm (28¾ x 51⁹⁄₁₆ in.). Purchase 2002 Helen McMahon Brady Cutting Fund 2002.1.33.

22. *Khaden* (bed rug), early twentieth century. Wool weft, cotton warp, natural dyes, 88 x 165 cm (34⅝ x 65 in.). Purchase 2002 Helen McMahon Brady Cutting Fund 2002.1.80.

Pomegranate Communications, Inc.
Box 808022, Petaluma CA 94975
800 227 1428
www.pomegranate.com

Pomegranate Europe Ltd.
Unit 1, Heathcote Business Centre, Hurlbutt Road
Warwick, Warwickshire CV34 6TD, UK
[+44] 0 1926 430111
sales@pomeurope.co.uk

1. *Shugden* (sitting rug). The wish-granting jewels in the dragon's claws represent rain.

2. Saddle rug. The peonies in this picture symbolize nobility.

3. Ceremonial appliquéd tent. The godly *khyung* is the rival of treasure-guarding serpents called *nagas*.

4. *Shugden*. The four fruits in the four corners symbolize abundance.

5. Lhamo's saddle cover. Around the Chinese yin-yang symbol is a *vishvavajra*, a symbol of stability.

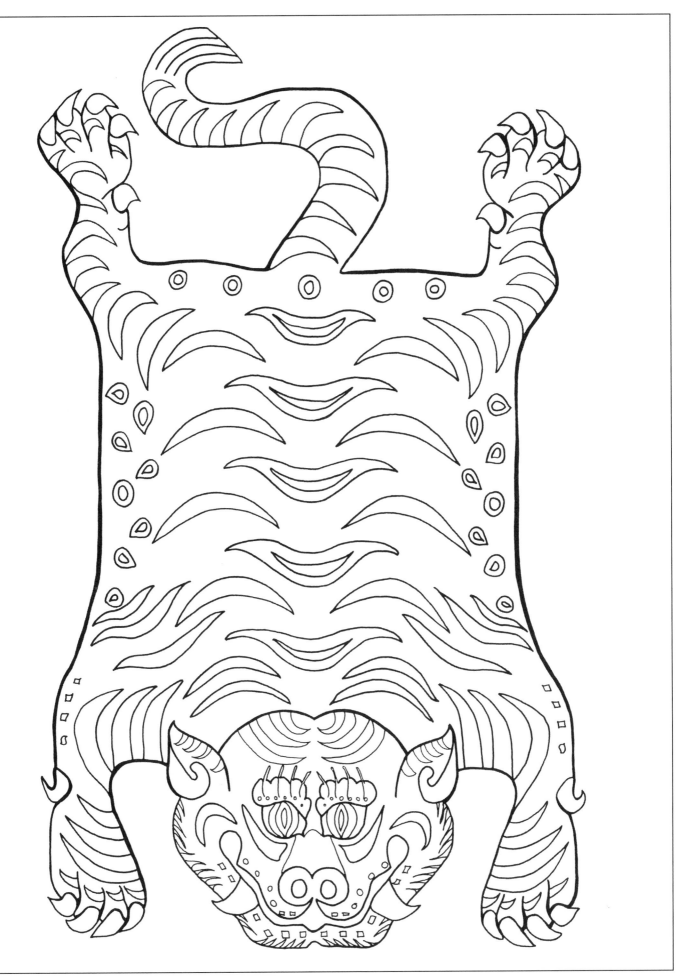

6. Tiger rug. The skin of the tiger represents spiritual power.

7. *Pema*. The lotus is a symbol of purity.

8. Door curtain rug. The vases stand for abundance, the endless knot (upper right) symbolizes eternity and continuity, and the shell (upper left) stands for sound and the unfolding universe.

9. *Shugden* (sitting rug). The angular border is a protective barrier.

10. *Kapsho pesar* ("Kapsho's new design"). Can you see some symbols you know?

11. Phoenix-pattern *khaden* (bed rug). Like dragons, phoenixes are virtuous and powerful.

12. Ritual table, side panel. The *kirtimukha* is a fierce guardian of celestial waters.

13. Altar canopy, Ngor Monastery. A Tibetan dragon flies among the clouds.

14. Gyabney (cushion cover). Lotus pendants dangle on either side of a hanging lantern.

15. Banner with "Face of Glory." Have you seen this fierce face before?

16. *Khaden* (bed rug). Butterflies and flowers suggest a regal garden.

17. *Khaden* (bed rug). A dragon and a phoenix, shown together, symbolize a happy married couple.

18. Saddle rug from Yabshi Phunkang's cavalry. The round Chinese character on this rug means "long life."

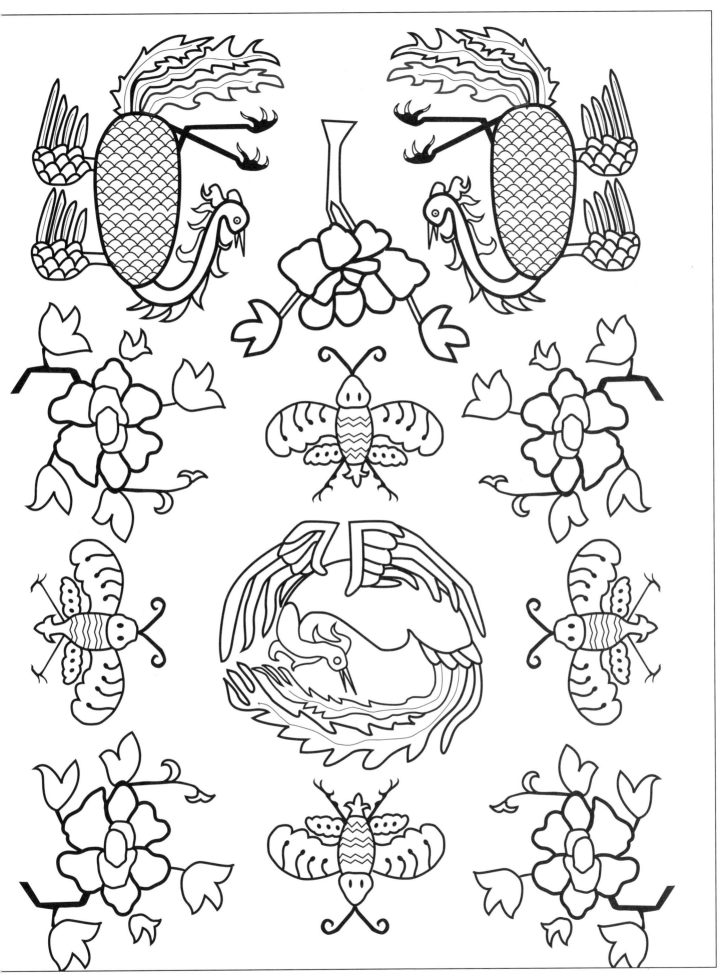

19. *Khaden* (bed rug). What living things do you see here beside the pheasant in the center?

20. Throne backrest. Below the *kirtimukha* is a pair of snow lions, who stand for joyous freedom.

21. *Pema chakdro* ("lotus in iron lockets").

22. *Khaden* (bed rug). The crane and pine tree are symbols of good fortune and long life.

Draw and color your own picture here!